Gilbert Haven

Te Deum Laudamus

The cause and the consequence of the election of Abraham Lincoln. A

Thanksgiving sermon.

Gilbert Haven

Te Deum Laudamus
*The cause and the consequence of the election of Abraham Lincoln. A Thanksgiving
sermon.*

ISBN/EAN: 9783337115722

Printed in Europe, USA, Canada, Australia, Japan

Cover: Foto ©Lupo / pixelio.de

More available books at **www.hansebooks.com**

THE

CAUSE AND THE CONSEQUENCE

OF THE

ELECTION OF ABRAHAM LINCOLN;

A

𝕿𝖍𝖆𝖓𝖐𝖘𝖌𝖎𝖇𝖎𝖓𝖌 𝖘𝖊𝖗𝖒𝖔𝖓

DELIVERED IN THE

Harvard St. M. E. Church, Cambridge, Sunday Evening, Nov. 11, 1860,

BY

REV. GILBERT HAVEN.

But as we were allowed of God to be put in trust with the Gospel, even so we speak; not as pleasing men, but God, which trieth our hearts. 1 THESS. i, 4.

BOSTON:

J. M. HEWES, PRINTER, 81 CORNHILL.

SOLD BY J. P. MAGEE, No. 5 CORNHILL.

1860.

HON. CHARLES SUMNER,

WHO has spoken the bravest words for Liberty in the most perilous places ; who has suffered in behalf of the Slave only less than those who wear the martyr's crown ; who has come forth from that suffering with the profoundest, because experimental, sympathy with the Oppressed, with a more intense hatred of the Oppression, yet without any bitterness of heart against the Oppressor ; who will stand forth in the future times as the clearest-eyed, boldest-tongued, and purest-hearted Statesman of the age,—these few words of Thanksgiving and Praise for the manifestation of the Presence and Power of the ALMIGHTY REDEEMER in this greatest work of our time, are most respectfully dedicated.

☞ The following discourse is published at the request of many who heard it. Candor requires us to say, what those who read it will naturally suppose, that it did not meet the approval of all the audience. Those who disagreed with it when spoken, we trust will find it less objectionable upon perusal and reflection. It would have been issued earlier had not illness prevented. Events have transpired since its delivery that might slightly modify some of the subordinate thoughts, but its leading positions, we still believe, to be true. A word of thanksgiving may not be untimely, when so many men's hearts are failing them through needless fear. The Spirit, through its servant, said unto the churches, when a far greater darkness closed around a far greater cause, "Rejoice, and again I say, rejoice." Shall not we then hail with rejoicings the sun of Equal Liberty, now rising upon our land, though tempestuous clouds suddenly rush across the glowing sky? They are clouds without water—clouds without the lightnings of death. With the brightness of its coming it will scatter all this darkness, calm all this tempest, and fill the whole nation with the blessed radiance of universal Liberty. The motto of our land, by God's goodness, shall ever be, as it has been, " LIBERTY AND UNION, NOW AND FOREVER, ONE AND INSEPARABLE."

CAMBRIDGE, DEC. 25, 1860.

DISCOURSE.

"I WILL SING UNTO THE LORD, FOR HE HATH TRIUMPHED GLORIOUSLY. THE HORSE AND HIS RIDER HATH HE THROWN INTO THE SEA." Exodus xv, 1.

"BUT PROMOTION COMETH NEITHER FROM THE EAST, NOR FROM THE WEST, NOR FROM THE SOUTH.

"BUT GOD IS JUDGE: HE PUTTETH DOWN ONE, AND SETTETH UP ANOTHER." Ps. lxxv, 6, 7.

"JESUS SAITH UNTO THEM, DID YE NEVER READ IN THE SCRIPTURES, THE STONE WHICH THE BUILDERS REJECTED, THE SAME IS BECOME THE HEAD OF THE CORNER: THIS IS THE LORD'S DOING, AND IT IS MARVELLOUS IN OUR EYES." Matt. xxi, 42.

ONE year ago last Sabbath evening, we assembled in this house to meditate on the beginning of the end of American Slavery. A fortnight before, a score of men had made a descent on a National Arsenal, freed some slaves, been captured by the soldiers of the Federal Government, their leader tried, condemned and sentenced to be hung. You well remember the month that followed—far more exciting than the one through which we have just passed. For thirty days, from Calais to Galveston, only one name was on every lip, only one feeling in every heart. You all remember the day of his death:

> "Sweet day, so cool, so calm, so bright,
> The bridal of the earth and sky."

You remember, far more clearly, the death itself,—more sweet, more cool, more calm, more bright, his soul's great bridal of earth and heaven. No death of greater beauty adorns the pages of secular history—no one sublimer is in the annals of Christian martyrdom. Socrates, with the hemlock at his lips, was not more charming and childlike. Latimer, in the fire, was not more cheerful. Paul, among the lions, was not more triumphant. It was by far the greatest death-scene in American history, and will shine forth purer and nobler with every passing year, and passing age.

A year has well nigh fled, and that life and death have been reviewed by me in such a fullness of immortal light as only the greatest sorrow can pour upon the soul. In that great light, his purpose and principles have only shone the purer, and I could not enter on the glorious subject of our present meditation, without repeating, as my maturest convictions, the approval my heart and your hearts then spontaneously uttered.

We come to-night not to sorrow over liberty enslaved afresh—liberty, tried by the jury of the country, and without cause, without consideration, found guilty—liberty under sentence of death and on her way to the scaffold. No, thanks be to God, the beginning of the end of slavery gives us gladder scenes in the opening of the second act of its fast accomplishing drama.

The defeat at Bunker's Hill and the death of Warren—a lost day and a lost leader, cast an immeasurable gloom, for a season, in spite of some redeeming features, over the American heart.* But the second great act, executed, like this, in but little less than a year from the first, executed, like this, under the leadership of the chosen captain of their hosts, by which a proud and mighty enemy, flushed with long success, and backed by the gigantic powers of a great nation, without the firing of a gun, evacuated their most important post in the whole country, left it, never to return,—the great deed by which Washington purged Boston of its insolent and murderous foe, thrilled the whole nation with unmitigated joy. So this peaceful evacuation by the arrogant, wealthy and long ruling Slave Power of the most important post it ever held or can hold, never to return, has caused such a flood of ecstacy as never before filled the hearts of this people, since the bells rang out the first declaration, and the bewildered multitudes

* See appendix A.

awoke to the realization of their existence as a united and free nation. The perplexing and saddening features of the event of last year do not mar this victory. No gallows tree stretches its black arms athwart the golden sky, no dying groans, no stiffened forms attend the triumphal shout and march. Shall we not, then, come before His presence with thanksgivings whose right hand and holy arm hath gotten Him the victory. For promotion cometh neither from the east, nor from the west, nor from the south. But God is judge: he putteth down one and setteth up another.

Not in the interest of the great party through whom He has done this work, do I appear, but in the interest of that cause which swells far, far beyond the power of that or any party to embrace,—the redemption of millions upon millions of my fellow men. In their behalf I raise the song of praise. That redemption draweth nigh. Power is passing away from the side of the oppressor. Power which belongeth unto God, is being employed by Him to break this infamous yoke. Shall we not laud and magnify his Name, in whose hand are the hearts of the children of men, that he has turned them as the rivers of water are turned, and made them sweep upon, soon we trust to sweep away, this rooted, and massy iniquity in their overflowing, swift rushing flood?

You may ask is it not a profanation of the sanctuary to employ it for rejoicings over mere political strifes? This is very far from an ordinary victory, and for its celebration we have the unanimous voice of all ages and all religions.

Abraham praised God in a temple not made with hands, for the defeat of his enemies, and Melchizedek, the priest of the most high God, the type of Christ, poured upon his head the divine benedictions. The victories of the Hebrew kings were celebrated in the temple, and some of the grandest psalms were written in praise of national deliverances. The heathen have followed this natural sentiment, and in all ages and nations have hung the trophies of their triumphs in their temples; have made their praises to their gods rise above their shouts over their fallen foe. So the Philistines rejoiced before Dagon, when they had captured Samson: and, in a later day, when they gained possession of the Ark of God. The history of Delphi and other templed spots is but a catalogue of such thanksgivings. The Christian world has, from the first, obeyed the ancestral, human law. "*Te, Deum laudamus*," "We praise thee, Oh God," has rung through the lofty arches of great cathedrals, and against the dome of heaven, for more than a thousand years, when the Lord had given their country deliverance in the day of battle.

We have, therefore, abundant precedent in the universal practice of our race for entering these courts, to-night, with thanksgivings, and these walls with praise. Have we abundant reason? It may be said that these religious national rejoicings were because of victories won on bloody fields, won over a foreign foe and at the expense of human life. Is a mere periodical strife, peaceful and bloodless, between brethren of the same family, for the honors of civil life, is this to be placed beside the overthrow of the Egyptians, the destruction of the Assyrians, the redemption of Europe at Waterloo, of Italy at Solferino? Is it not straining a point to thus elevate the mad whirl of quadrennial politics into a great national, a great world battle, which marks an epoch in the history of the race?

These questions are very proper. For if it be but the ordinary strife of ordinary politics, although the Church has the guardianship of these as she has of every other matter pertaining to human duty, yet she might safely leave them to the general course of her counsel and authority, without making their ephemeral victories subject of especial exultation.

Let us then ask, as a needful preliminary to our songs of gladness and of hope, what was the subject of controversy in the late conflict?

The only subject set before the people was slavery; its extension and nationalization, or its relegation to the regions now blackened with it, there to

"writhe in pain,
And die amid its worshippers."

Four parties were professedly in the field, but only two combatants,—only one question. In different parts of the land, the two intermediate parties took different positions according to the sentiment ruling there. In the South they contended against the domineering passion for the national supremacy of Slavery. In the North they fought with equal zeal against its ruling passion, the national supremacy of Liberty. Their bands flew across the field, now striking at the haughty slave power, and now, at the iron legions of Freedom.

Behind them advanced steadily the great hosts with their banners flying, each glowing with its one word. On the one side the gorgeous black flag—upon it, lurid flames shooting forth that word infernal, Slavery. On the other, the lustrous white flag, "so as no fuller on earth can whiten," with the *logos* celestial, Liberty, flashing from its radiant folds. Marching beneath them, each party felt, instinctively, immeasurably felt, that the issue involved the most vital questions ever submitted to this nation ; and, that the result was sure to be disastrous to freedom, if defeated, fatal to slavery, if it should go down in the battle.

No other question was debated by the leading advocates of all parties. One of the candidates for the Presidency, and one of the ablest men in the country, traversed its length and breadth, making many addresses ; and the burden of every one was Slavery. True he endeavored to exclude it from the canvass, but he could not exclude it from his own speeches. It rounded every sentence, pointed every line. And it was not a little remarkable that so sagacious a statesman should not have perceived, that what had filled all his public life, good and evil, for a decade of years, was not to be banished from the general mind, nor settled in the national councils, except by a fair fight on the appointed field.

The other party, though attempting to banish it from their platform, showed the impossibility of the attempt in its very phraseology. For its two chief words, " Constitution and Union," proved that they felt or fancied these to be endangered by the struggle with slavery. Its worthy appendix, "the enforcement of the laws," was aimed solely at the execution of the most unchristian and inhuman act that ever issued from a Christian legislature. If it were not so, I hope that other law for the suppression of the sale of intoxicating liquors, which especially

2

needs enforcement in this section, will be executed by this locally large and influential party. They will find enough who disagree with them as to the duty of enforcing the Fugitive Slave Act, who will gladly aid them in executing the most excellent of Massachusetts laws in her rum-ridden metropolis.

From the unwilling, but universal confession of neutrals, therefore, no less than from the declarations of real opponents, do we see clearly the field of conflict. The real weapons of the real fighters were all drawn from one armory, all waged in one battle. The only speaker that advocated the Southern party in this region made the strongest defence of human slavery ever made in Massachusetts. There was an honest boldness that was refreshing to witness, in inviting Mr. Yancey to give a pro-slavery speech in Faneuil Hall—a boldness no party would have been equal to in any previous campaign. The invitation was not accepted by a timid man. No abler, no bolder speech was ever made in Boston than Mr. Yancey's, viewed as a eulogy on a system abhorrent in the utmost degree to almost every one of his audience. As he was here, so were his associates every where on slave soil. As he was here, so would the advocates of freedom have been, had they been allowed to speak in Richmond, Charleston, Mobile or New Orleans. So were they on their native heather, the broad free soil of the North.

Not a syllable was breathed against the candidate of slavery, except his devotion to that system ; not a syllable against the victorious leader of the hosts of Freedom, except his opposition to it. " It is the cause," then, " it is the cause, my friends," that has organized, inspired, waged and won this national battle. It is the cause, too, that commands me to speak to-night, to speak in my official capacity, as an ambassador of Jesus Christ, upon one of the especial objects of my mission—the freedom, equality and fraternity of the human race.

Some may yet complain that we drag the holy vestments of the altar in this mire of social strife. Do you remember how Phinehas, the priest of the Most High God, possibly while arrayed in most sacred robes, and, in his hand, the sacrificial knife consecrated exclusively to the service of the altar, rushed in among the sinning Israelites and their idolatrous associates, slaying heathen and Hebrew in the midst of their profane abominations? And do you remember how that Most High God said to Moses, " Phinehas, the son of Eleazer, the son of Aaron, the priest, hath turned my wrath away from the children of Israel, while he was zealous for my sake among them, that I consumed not the children of Israel in my jealousy. Wherefore say, Behold I give unto him my covenant of peace : And he shall have it and his seed after him, even the covenant of an everlasting priesthood : because he was zealous for his God and made an atonement for the children of Israel." Was it a greater deed for this minister to stay the plague of voluntary passion, than for us to seek to stay that plague which makes pure and pious men and women the victims of every conceivable lust that power, avarice or passion breeds ?

If Christ showed that the zeal of the house of the Lord had eaten him up, by scourging from the temple, the seat of civil as well as religious authority, those that sold doves, shall we say his servants are not his followers, when they seek to scourge from our temple of civil and religious liberty those that sell MEN ? The temple of our national life has become defiled. Woe to that priest who is dumb before the defilers ! In Christ's day some of them shared in the business that profaned his house. In our day some of them share in the honors and profits of this far greater profanation. Let us obey the example he has set us,— not the decrees of timid, time-serving, wicked men.

But this defence is unnecessary before this congregation. The contest as to the rights and duties of the ministry to engage in this work has long been settled in this region. Here and there, the rare exceptions requisite to prove a rule rise before us, denying the privileges of humanity to those who are set to apply to the hearts of men all the laws of the Divine Author of humanity. Not so with the multitudes. Slavery is to them an object not only of civil, but of religious detestation. Its defeat, on any field, is a cause of religious thanksgiving. Its defeat on the field where it has just fallen,—the field it has ruled the longest and the ablest, where its chief seat is by choice, and by necessity if it retain any seat in the land, its overthrow and its expulsion from the throne of the national government, its flight to its native lair, and the soon coming fight there for bare existence, these are subjects of the most devout, the most rapturous praise. "Not unto us, O Lord, not unto us, but unto thy name give glory, for thy mercy and thy truth's sake."

Let us, then, gratefully meditate on the late victory, considering its cause and its consequence.

I. *Its Cause. Why has Freedom triumphed?*

For two chief reasons among a multitude of lesser ones; First, the growth of conscience as to the nature and effects of slavery; and, Second, the growth of fear as to its political power and prospects.

The first and profoundest cause is the awakening of the conscience of the nation as to the dreadful character and workings of slavery.

There must always be two periods, at least, of attack upon any organized iniquity before the tide of moral sentiment deluges and drowns it forever. The first awakening is moderately efficient, but the mighty sin is too strong for complete overthrow. The besieging hosts get weary and slumber on their arms. The enemy sallies forth and triumphs over them. They dwell in captivity to the evil they rose against. Again the conscience grows, again the vice is attacked, and in the new assault is left weaker than before, perhaps completely destroyed; if not, the victorious right yields anew to the slumber of sloth and sin; is chained and ruled afresh, again bursts its bands and sweeps on irresistibly to victory. Thus, by tidal waves of flux and reflux, the huge mountain of sin is finally buried beneath the deep, abounding ocean of truth.

So the Jews moved forward, from Joshua to David, in the subjugation of Canaan. So Christianity has marched, is marching forward in the subjugation of the world. So Grecian idolatry, in a hand to hand fight with early Christianity, fell and rose, fell and rose, weaker at each resurrection, till three hundred years after its first defeat, that form, eminent and potent for more than a thousand years, fell, never to rise again. So Roman slavery staggered and tumbled before the sharp blows of the same Apostolic

Christianity,—sprang to its feet with the ferocity and strength of a wounded lion and rent its enemies in pieces ; again felt the shafts, again reeled and fell, again rose and raged, till, after half a millennium, the golden rule of the Saviour and the golden command of his apostle to Christian masters, to give their servants that which was just and equal, were finally obeyed, and throughout Christian Europe, property in man passed into the execrable list, abjured and abominated by every person.

The black race, in consequence of its seclusion and degradation, was separated almost entirely from this influence. True, Africa had been honored with the earliest, and, in many respects, the ablest of Christian schools. Her sons had worn the consecrated mitre, and sat in equal authority with the Bishops of Rome and Jerusalem in Episcopal Councils. But the ravages of the Vandals nipped this budding civilization, and Mussulman fanaticism perpetuated the work northern Paganism had achieved.

Christian Europe, hemmed in by Mohammedanism on the south and south-east, and by the wildest heathenism on the north and north-east, without extensive commerce and without mechanic arts, itself the child of northern idolatry, baptized with the childish Christianity of Rome, grew, by slow and unequal steps, to a true manhood in Christ. So far had she retrograded from her earliest faith in the last two centuries, that traffic in human flesh was again found among her lawful commerce. And though she never fell back so far as to acknowledge the right of property in the white and Christian man, she did finally recognize the idea of ownership in the African race.

It was reserved for this land to inaugurate the work of universal emancipation. That work began with the beginning of our history, and has risen and fallen, with mingled success and failure, to the victory of this hour. Massachusetts first refused to receive a cargo of slaves at the same time that Virginia first welcomed them. The principles involved in those two deeds have been in conflict, violent or latent, throughout our whole history.

The fundamental law, on which universal personal freedom must stand, the law of perfect equality before God, has long been settled here, has never yet been acknowledged elsewhere in the world. America was settled by the flower of Protestantism before it had fallen into the scar and yellow leaf of formalism, or the thrice dead infidelity which covered all Europe, Protestant and Catholic, in the last century, with thorns and briars fit only for cursing.

Our fathers, the Pilgrims and Puritans of Massachusetts, the Baptists of Rhode Island, the Quakers and Lutherans of Pennsylvania, the Episcopalians of Virginia, the Catholics of Maryland, and the Huguenots of Carolina, were all refugees from religious persecution. Every State was settled or largely populated by sufferers for conscience sake. And after a few ineffectual struggles to employ the same cramps and fetters upon others that had been visited upon themselves, they arose, one after another, to the true apprehension of the rights of conscience, and Puritan and Episcopalian, Baptist and Pedobaptist, Quaker and Lutheran, Huguenot and Catholic, came to that broad table land of universal freedom to the religious sentiment which is still the most wonderful characteristic of this nation.

So thoroughly had this doctrine filled the air of common life, long before the formation of our confederacy, that only the briefest and most incidental reference to the whole subject is found in our Constitution. I have heard a scholarly Englishman complain of it for this very defect—a defect like that found in the Bible, where proofs of the existence of God, and the obligations of Religion are never given, its every line assuming these as accredited, universal truths.

So did our fathers settle the other great question—the greatest that affects our human relations—the absolute right of every man to himself. Advancing, not ascending, on the lofty table land of the equality of every man before God, they stood upon that first of human truths—the equality of every man before his fellows. While Europe bowed down to certain families and individuals as royal and sovereign by right divine, and, as a natural consequence, esteemed the other extreme of society, whether peasants or slaves, as void of all rights which the crouchers were bound to respect, the American people, coming together, through their representatives, themselves the nominal holders of slaves, unanimously, unhesitatingly, enthusiastically declared that " All men are created free and equal." Such a declaration by the founders of a nation the world had never heard before.

Their first struggle was to establish their own equality before King, and Nobles, and Parliament, and a haughty people. They must prove the fallacy of the divine right of kings on the battle-field. Only one great inspiration can possess at a time, a man or a people. This broad platform must rest on the head of king and slaveholder, but it must be planted on that of the king first, as the most imminent and dangerous foe. Hence the revolutionary struggle and victory.

When they had emerged from that conflict—when George the Third saluted George Washington, and, through him, the American people, as his perfect equal, then came a second duty—to preserve this equality among themselves. How perilous was their state you can faintly conceive, by seeing how all classes have just been swept into the current of an unnatural reverence for the youthful heir of that throne.

These patriots were born royalists. A vast proportion of the people were, in feeling and theory, royalists. Every city was full of wealth and fashion thus devoted. If England's royalty and nobility were expelled, might not America substitute one of her own ? Italy has just proved the passion of a people for a king. Mazzini and Garibaldi had to yield to Victor Emanuel, republic-anism to royalty. So might it have been here. Our fathers saved us by self-denial. It was a greater work to deliver them-selves from themselves than from England. " Greater is he that ruleth his spirit than he that taketh a city."

Every member of that Constitutional Convention could have had an American title of nobility. Lands for the support of that title were more abundant than William's barons found them in Eng-land in the eleventh century. The leaders of the people, Wash-ington, Hamilton, Adams, and Jefferson, would have been of the blood royal or next the throne. They saw the peril. They must meet it. They did. They especially guarded against inequality of rank, forbad the receipt of titles from foreign courts, and steered clear of the currents that might sweep them into that channel—a senate without pay or for life, an executive for life or for a long term of years. And they consumated their precautions by one of their earliest acts of legislation—forbidding the increase of the Society of the Cincinnati, or even its continuance among the sons of the original members, as this society, being composed of the officers of the Revolution, might, through the fascination of the military spirit, endanger their primal and most vital idea—equality, liberty.

As we have said, only one fever can rage at a time, only one great duty be done at once. Therefore, while their sympathies went out for the slave population, while their conscience told them they should be equally faithful and honest to these as to themselves, their exhausting labors were in another direction. They rested from their labors, fondly hoping their children would take up and apply their great principles to this oppressed people.

Of the chief revolutionary patriots, Franklin alone was an avowed abolitionist. Jefferson wrote against slavery, or rather wrote reflections upon it, but never worked vigorously for its extinction. Franklin cast his influence on that side, probably, more because he dwelt among the liberty-loving Quakers than from an inherent passion of his own. Washington disliked it, but when urged by Lafayette to make the experiment of emancipating and hiring his negroes, he declines on account of the embarrassed state of his property, and yet he died shortly after, leaving an estate estimated at half a million of dollars, which is more than a million at the present valuation of money.

The fact must be stated that while faithful to one half of their theory, they were practically indifferent to the other. While abolishing all titular distinctions and equalizing all the white inhabitants, they failed to abolish the title of slaveholder, and to give their colored brethren that which was just and equal.

The battle on this field exhausted all their energies. To keep this liberty from licentiousness, this equality from familiarity, to preserve an aristocracy, to sustain democracy against aristocracy, to secure state rights, to maintain the federal unity and strength, on these important fields the war raged, and the servant of servants was unnoticed in his servitude among the great questions of social and political equality that so violently agitated the governing classes.

This work was perhaps as much as one age could do. It was certainly more than any one age had previously done. The men who achieved it were more than thirty years in accomplishing it. Thomas Jefferson wrought wondrously for the rights of man, from 1776 to 1809—thirty-three years of most remarkable service in a most remarkable cause. He was then past sixty—an old man, weary with the cares of State—not fit in vigor or vehemence for the great work of emancipation. Failing to keep progressive he slid backwards, and dishonored his gray hairs by apologizing for slavery and defending the Missouri compromise.

The generation that succeeded them, as great men's sons are apt to be, were very poor imitators of their illustrious fathers. Most trees bear only biennially. Most generations are under a similar law. A great calm follows a great storm. The children of these revolutionary parents were feeble in principle, low in moral tone. They were tired of great ideas and great deeds. The overstrained nature sprang back to the narrower range which men naturally prefer. The leading men of that age, men who have just left us, were far below their fathers in greatness of nature, and will be incalculably beneath them in greatness of fame. Clay, Calhoun, Adams, Webster and Jackson, its five representative men, present to the historian no such lofty traits of character or service as shine in the names of five representatives of the preceding era, Washington, Adams, Jefferson, Hamilton and Franklin.

John Quincy Adams alone of his peers held forth the light that glowed in his youth. But not he, till he had descended from the presidental throne into the vale of age and comparative political obscurity. Hardly a word of his can be quoted before his seventieth year, that has the ringing sound of liberty. How different from the *young John* Adams in the mass meetings of Boston, the provincial Congress and Independence Hall. Fortunate was he that those last few years and that congressional opportunity were given him.

It was an era of the deadening of the conscience, on the sub-

3

ject of freedom. Church and State alike fell into the slumber. Political and religious compromises became the order of the day. The *sentiment* of the fathers was against slavery. But sentiment can do nothing against sin. And so the sons came to endure, to pity, to embrace the unclean thing, and from Calhoun to Webster, fell down and worshipped the abominable idol their pious fathers had neglected to destroy.

"New times demand new measures and new men."

The new times had arrived. New men, and their new measures were not wanting. The third generation appears on the stage of action. The grandsires find their likeness in their grand-children, not their children. Thirty years passed from the triumph of Jefferson to that of Jackson, the representatives of the ideas of their generations. Thirty years have passed from the triumph of Jackson to that of the Anti-Slavery sentiment, not in the person of its recognized exponent, but still in the strength of its mighty feeling and purpose. This thirty years covers the era of this agitation, covers the adult life of its promoters. You will find on the Liberator of this year, "Volume XXX:" and this sheet has the honor of initiating the movement in this nation.

The conscience was aroused very slowly. The deadly slumber was pleasant. Churches, societies, parties, every body disliked to be disturbed. But the young men sympathized with young Mr. Garrison and his young idea. Young Mr. Seward then emerging into public life, felt the throbbings of the new inspiration. Young Mr. Phillips and Mr. Sumner, then students at Harvard or on their way thither; the youthful Tappan, and Leavitt, and Lovejoy, and Giddings, and Gerritt Smith, caught the flame in their fresh and sympathetic hearts, and commenced kindling it in the breasts of others. Dr. Channing and John Quincy Adams were almost the only men of accomplished fame that endorsed the enterprise, and they did not publicly coöperate with its youthful managers.

Soon bitter conflicts sprang up in the breasts of these young philanthropists. The fresh armed men began to bite and devour one another, and were well nigh consumed one of another. Yet still the great inspiration moved on, through them, in spite of them. New measures were required by the progress of the sentiment. The conscience growing, demanded a chance to express itself at the ballot box. This was resisted by Mr. Garrison. He did more than this. Led by his love of free speech, he permitted some of his leading associates to burden the " *animosus infans* " with gross infidelities and social absurdities. But its intense life threw off all these deformities. Would that, in his sphere of effort, and to the measure of his large abilities and influence, he had kept this liberty from becoming licentiousness. Would that he, like Wilberforce, had kept his heart sweet with prayer and piety through the whole of this great war. Wiser minds, not larger hearts, took the reins ; or, rather, on different parts of the same field, with different weapons, they fought the common foe.

This conscience has thus steadily increased until this hour. The vast majority of the men of to-day have grown up under its power ; for the mass of men are under forty-five years. The impressible youth of fifteen, who drank of this new wine when it was first pressed from the grapes of a fresh experience, is to-day the governor elect of your commonwealth. The poor youth of twenty, toiling in the solitude of western rivers and forests, learning to abhor slavery because of its contempt for honorable industry, is to-day the civil leader of the cause and country.

Thus has the conscience which moved our grandsires to the great work of personal liberation, moved us towards the completion of their work, in the liberation of more persons than their valor saved, from a bondage infinitely worse than that which pressed them down.

But, secondly, fears created by the rapid march of the slave power have aided in this work. The growth of this power has been a necessary complement of the corresponding growth of the abolition sentiment. The Gospel is a savor of life unto life and of death unto death. Conscience is one and the same in every man. But conscience trampled upon, is sure to revenge itself by allowing the passions that expel it from its seat to assume a diabolic sovereignty. The Southern mind felt as keenly as the Northern that slavery was a sin. There was but one testimony from the whole land in our early history, and even as late as the beginning of this agitation. But when the conscience began to be heard saying, clearly, "extirpate this evil. Let my oppressed go free and break every yoke."—self interest said "Nay. I shall impoverish myself by so doing. My money is invested in slaves. My habits and tastes are educated in slavery. My heart inclines to it." So they resisted the Spirit of God. They trampled under foot the national life-principle. They counted the revolutionary blood shed for them an unholy thing. They turned and rent those who cast these pearls at their feet, and who called upon them to adorn their brows with their lustre.

They began to defend the system through the press, in the forum, on the bench, from the pulpit. They sought to extend it. They sought to open the accursed trade which should populate their wildernesses with the barbaric merchandise. They enthroned themselves in the national legislature, in the presidental chair, in the supreme court. They trod out freedom of the press, freedom of speech, almost freedom of thought, in all the slave States. They were on the point of nationalizing slavery in the territories, in every free State. Their children, fifty years hence, will not believe their fathers zealously advocated practices so abhorrent to human nature.

There was no real change in the Southern conscience. That still told them "You are verily guilty concerning your brother." "Slavery is the sum of all villanies." I never saw a slaveholder who did not, when he spoke his real sentiments, make this confession.

A gentleman who long lived in Alabama told me he had often heard slaveholders, worth a million of this property, say, "The slaves have just as much right to their freedom, as I, to mine." It was this conscience that made the whole South shake with indistinguishable terror, when they heard that hero-martyr saying to their bondmen "You are as free as I or your master. Here is a weapon to defend yourself if they attempt to enslave you. Here is one who will aid you in using that weapon, if they dare to attack you." Their audacious course consummated its malignity in the murder of that man whom every one of them knew was in the right and doing right. For they saw, however blind we might be, that he was of the blood royal of mankind, most of whom rule the race from the scaffold. They felt that he was proving in this deed, his lineal descent from the patriotic but defeated Gracchii, and Demosthenes, and Wallace, and Hampden, and Vane, and Russell. But time would fail me to mention the grand list of martyrs for liberty into whose front ranks they saw him enter, who all died in the faith, not inheriting the promises.

This God-defying march of the hosts of Satan upon the sacred institutions, the more sacred inspirations of the land, helped to stimulate the already quickening conscience of the North. The heaviest eyes began to open—the dullest natures to stir. Every one whose heart throbbed with any of the life of their fathers, of their fathers' God, felt that the evil must be rebuked, must be repressed, must be extirpated, so far as any constitutional or moral power could do it. So the Church and the State have moved together,—here, slowly and cautiously, there boldly and manfully, every where motion, every where life, until the mighty work is wrought which puts our government, openly and entirely, on the side of Freedom.

This then is the cause, this alone—the Spirit of God moving on the hearts of the children of men. " This is the Lord's doing, and it is marvellous in our eyes." " Not unto us, O Lord, not unto us, but unto Thy name give glory." The Lord hath triumphed gloriously. " The horse and his rider," the Northern political slave and his Southern political master, " hath He cast into the sea."

II. *Let us now consider the consequence of this victory, which is one in fact, though threefold in form.*

First. It will suppress all efforts to extend slavery. The battle was waged at this point. Here, too, was it won. For the first time in all this long conflict the hostile parties agreed as to the object in dispute. Every previous Democratic Convention shut off the real issue from the people. The Whig and American parties, when alive, were equally careful. Tariff, banks, the Catholic question, retrenchment and reform, all these have turned away the gaze of the masses from their real danger and duty. Mr. Douglas supposed that what had been, would still be, and therefore attempted to get up a war-cry that should mean nothing, while under its delusion, the people should again put in power their haughty tyrant. But the honesty of the slave power swept away this subterfuge. They boldly placed at the head of their columns the universal supremacy of slavery. The free sentiment hailed the conflict. The deadly embrace is passed, and slavery lies prone upon the field. A tyrant once slain is slain forever. Error can never survive its Waterloo. Freedom had often fallen, but it rose ever the more beautiful and strong from its momentary defeat. Slavery has fallen, never to rise again defiant, successful. It will rule in New York and Boston before it ever rules again at Washington. It ruled there first only by our consent. We must rehabilitate it at home before we allow it to return thither.

This absolute and unquestioned gain—the point, the centre of the fight is almost incalculable. Some speak slightingly of it and say nothing is done. The Fugitive Slave act is recognized by President Lincoln as constitutional. He will favor the admission of slave states if they come constitutionally to the door of the nation. These are not agreeable sights. Yet, consider how unlikely they are to occur. What slave state will seek admission to an Anti-Slavery confederacy? As for the fugitive from slavery, unless vital modifications are made in the present law, the people will take care that he is not returned. Can one here be seized, and sentenced to bondage again as unrighteously as Anthony Burns was, and pass down State street in broad daylight, fettered by a squad of foreign mercenaries, when more than a hundred thousand of the citizens of Massachusetts have put the most eloquent defender of the Personal Liberty bill in the chair of State?

The accursed oceanic slave trade will forever cease. New York will be relieved from the miserable honor of sending out these vessels,—Savannah and Charleston, the more miserable honor of receiving their cargoes. Africa and Cuba will be girdled with a moving wall of fire through which but few of the dreadful craft can pass. If nothing more were done than is assuredly done, it is wonderful, it is worthy of unbounded thanksgivings.

But, secondly, we have done still more. We have set ourselves right before the world. We shall cast our influence, as a great nation, on the side of universal liberty. For years we have been a by-word and a hissing among the nations. Not a word for freedom could escape the lips of our representatives abroad, for they were bound, hand and foot, mouth and tongue, with the graveclothes of this body of death. Our influence has been against freedom every where, in every man. The conscience of the slaveholder, the conscience of the tyrants of France and Austria and Rome, were stifled in the deadly air which our government exhaled. All this is changed. America will stand forth in the glory of her earlier, better days;—in a glory greater than that, for we now appear as the upholder of the rights of every man, of every hue and condition. Italians contend for the rights of Italians, Hungarians for Hungarians, Englishmen for Englishmen ; we, alone, for the black race, the weakest and least favored of the children of Adam. Napoleon boasted that he went to war for an idea. We fought for vastly more,—the foundation principle of humanity,—the oneness in blood and destiny of the human race.

This influence is worth every thing. It is irrepressible. it is unavoidable. The acts and words of the Administration will be most careful and moderate, but this power it cannot repress. It is an ANTI-SLAVERY Government. It was created because it was anti-slavery. That word assures us that a new life is breathed into the soul of the nation. It will thrill with its enthusiasm every section of the land, every corner of the globe. Distracted Mexico will now turn entreating eyes upon us, certain to see no wolfish leer in our gaze, hungering to reduce her citizens to slaves. The South American Republics will sit at our feet, and follow our footsteps in the upward march to perfect freedom. Hayti will stand at our capitol among the great nations, its representative sitting with those of England and France, in the seats of ambassadorial dignity and equality. Italy and France, Germany and England, will, as never before, admire and imitate the mistress of nations, sitting in the glory of universal liberty on the highest seat of earthly authority.

What is better than all, the sweet, summer morning air of freedom will once more steal over the hot and arid plains of southern despotism. Blowing from the whole north, through Washington, through the Executive mansion, it will nerve with vigor many a soul now paralyzed with fear. The minister of Christ, who has there, for these many years, denied his Master, will weep bitterly, and speak earnestly against the fearful crime that has so long cursed the church and his own soul. Literature will feel it. Southern Whittiers will arise, who shall make her hills and glades echo with their trumpet blasts of denunciation, their trumpet calls to the conflict and the victory. Mrs. Stowes will spring from their own soil, who will portray the evils and wrongs of their cherished " institution," the duty and blessedness of universal emancipation, in colors that shall outshine their marvellous prototype, because they will be drawn from personal experiences, and filled with the enthusiasm that only such experiences can inspire. The whole people will be made alive with the mighty wind, blowing from the hills of God over their fields of dry bones, and they shall stand upon their feet, an exceeding great army, for freedom.

What is already seen on the northern border of the black abyss will be seen every where. St. Louis gives almost ten thousand votes for liberty, as many as Boston, and, better than Boston, with these votes sends a bold and earnest abolitionist to the national councils. Baltimore gives over a thousand votes for freedom,—as many as the whole State of Massachusetts gave twenty years ago. That thousand has become a hundred thousand here in a score of years. It will become thrice that there, ere half that time has passed. In every southern city, even Charleston, the worst, will be found representatives of an anti-slavery government. In every State, papers will be advocating its principles ; in every heart the Spirit of God, which is liberty, will assert its claims, acknowledged, be obeyed. And that serpent, in whose folds a great multitude of Laocoöns are writhing in unspeakable agony, " that great serpent, which is the Devil and Satan," shall be bound, shall be hurled into the bottomless pit, shall disappear from this first and best of lands, and, with it, from the earth, forever.

For, lastly, this glorious victory assures the speedy abolition of slavery. I say, speedy, not with a few months, or a Presidential term in view, but with only a few years, in comparison with its long life and wide dominion.

The knell of slavery was struck last year in the heroic deed, and more heroic death of John Brown. He first shook the tottering Bastile to its foundations. It had been riddled, it had been undermined, but it had not rocked on its base till he put his hand upon it. It reeled to and fro like a slave ship in a storm, and well nigh foundered then. I have frequently mentioned this event with words of approval, such as but few, probably, in this audience will re-echo. It is proper, therefore, that I should pause and give a brief reason for my opinions. Our satirical neighbor says the millennium is near at hand,

" When preachers tell us all they think."

I have not shunned to declare to you the whole counsel of God on the highest of our duties. I shall not play the hypocrite now. Allowing the largest liberty of opinion to others, I claim equal liberty for myself. I know how the tide of misconception and condemnation still sets against Capt. Brown. I know that the Tribune and Independent,—anti-slavery journals of deserved influence,—still speak of his attempt as a " raid," a term of disparagement, if not of reproach. I know Mr. Seward said he was " justly hung." I know that many cry out with horror at the bare idea of putting weapons in the hands of the slaves, to maintain their freedom, and say, that he that apologizes for such an act defiles his sacerdotal garments and is become a companion with murderers.

But, on the other hand, I see how Victor Hugo and the other great and pure patriots of Europe can find no words to express their admiration of the deed and its doer. Struggling in chains of despotism at home, they know how to appreciate the intense humanity of one, who strove not to save himself, but others from a far worse tyranny than crushes them down. I see the strong

4

arm of Massachusetts wielding a sword, while she pronounces the sentence first uttered by the slaughtered patriot, Algernon Sydney, which might have been properly emblazoned, with Virginia's motto, on John Brown's banners, "*Ense petit placidam sub libertate quietem,*"—She seeks, with the sword, serene quiet under liberty. I see Hayti, the only really independent and enterprising African State, hailing the man with a spontaneous, reverence and admiration, and out of her poverty sending to his family thousands of dollars, as a token of her gratitude.

I find nothing in human nature, human history, or the Word of God that rebukes this sentiment. The gospel of Peace does not always require of its disciples non-resistance to every form of revolting oppression, but sometimes demands of them a stern resistance even "unto blood, striving against sin."

The Saviour himself, among his last injunctions, commands those of his disciples who had no sword, to sell their tunic, or chief garment, and buy one;—thereby clearly teaching us, that the clothing needful for the protection of our bodies is not to be placed beside the means of *defending* our liberties and our lives. This enterprise, as we understand it, sought to put the sword in the hands of the slave, *only* that he might *defend* his God-given freedom against his enslavers. So deep and universal is the conviction of this right, that had the people whom he strove to deliver been of our own race, or even of any race but the African, whom we hold in such inhuman contempt, there would have been no more objection to the *rightfulness* of the enterprise, than there was to the many unsuccessful attempts of our fathers to release their brethren from the far less terrible slavery, in which they were held by the Corsairs of Algiers.

In the light of these facts and principles, I find no condemnation for this man or his deed. In the light of its influence on the hideous wrong it assailed, I see much in it to approve. I cannot but conclude, therefore, that the words of censure so rife at present are the offspring of long indulged prejudice, or when uttered by some of our wise leaders, have been prompted either by an unwise desire to commend the anti-slavery chalice to the lips of slaveholders, by removing some of the bitter but essential

27

ingredients that strengthen the potion, or else by the temptations of ambition,—

> " That last infirmity of noble minds."

In either case they will yet be regretted more than any other of their utterances.

If this be called fanaticism I am content to bear the imputation. I am not alone in this state, however it may be elsewhere, if the late election truly expresses the sentiment of the people. The election to the governorship, by the largest vote any candidate ever received, of the man, who, more than all others, labored to save him from that " just" death, who publicly endorsed his character, if not the abstract rightfulness of the attempt, such an elevation of his best friend to our best office, is a strong evidence that our common sense and common humanity are getting the better of our fears and prejudices. The hated Mordecai already descends, here, from the gallows of public condemnation on which the Haman of a subtle pro-slaveryism had hung him, and rides through our streets in the royal apparel of executive sovereignty, as the man whom the people delighteth to honor. As if to show that this remarkable act of the people of Massachusetts was not the blind following of blind political leaders, but a silent yet real voice of approval, her favorite lyric poet comes forth and places a garland of exquisite beauty and perfume on the grave of the hero. Under the influence of his religious training, the Quaker Whittier cast upon his coffin a hastily gathered wreath of bitter herbs. But true also to the fundamental principles of his faith, through the influences of the events and reflections of the past year, he has discovered the " Inner Light" of superior truth, and with characteristic frankness, has published the revelations of that Light. A late poem, written on the liberation of Italy, by its own confession, covers the whole ground of the present controversy. The laurel which he places on Garibaldi's brow, he hangs alike on John Brown's tomb. Hear the sentiment of almost every Christian in these true and tender and solemn words :—

> " I dreamed of Freedom slowly gained
> By Martyr meekness, patience, faith.

And lo! an athlete grimly stained,
With corded muscles battle-strained,
Shouting it from the field of death!

* * * * * *

I know the pent fire heaves the crust,
That sultry skies the bolt will form
To smite them clear; that nature *must*
The balance of her powers adjust,
Though with the earthquake, and the storm.

And who am I, whose prayers would stay
The solemn recompense of time,
And lengthen Slavery's evil day
That outraged Justice may not lay
Its hand upon the sword of crime!

God reigns, and let the earth rejoice!
I bow before His sterner plan.
Dumb are the organs of my choice;
He speaks in battle's stormy voice,
His praise is in the wrath of man!"

If the violent act of one man thus paralyzed this iniquity, much more will the peaceful act of two millions tend to its annihilation. Our righteous and peaceful course will not be instantly answered in a similar spirit. It may at first, it undoubtedly will, intensify the rage that already burns in their breasts, seven-fold hotter than it did aforetime. This rage and fear will gnash upon us with its teeth, will seek to frighten us, by financial crises and threats of secession, into submission. Let us not be alarmed. Let but Wall street look on and hold on, calm and cool, as Menelaus did when Proteus sought to elude him by assuming terrific shapes and making beastly noises, and the monster now as then, will become tame and humble. Our greatest danger is in the cowardice of the moneyed power. The Church is getting ready to do her part, Politics is doing hers, and now the third of our social forces must do hers. If she fails, if she whines and grows pallid and begs her dear slaveholding brethren to desist, and promises northern repentance and its meet works, she will only encourage them in their course. She can *never* change the course of the Republic. Freedom is more than trade, liberty than wealth. Our fathers have said so twice. We shall not fail to repeat the word, if it must be spoken.

The poor slave will also burn in the hot breath of this fiery furnace. The master fears his slave more than he hates the North. He will feel the scourge of that fear. It is one of the necessities of tyrants that they can preserve their power, and even their life, only by the frequent deaths of their enslaved subjects. Sicilian prisons, Neapolitan dungeons, Roman inquisitions, every where, every when, has triumphant sin taught us that this necessity is laid upon it. So it is now where this worst of sins holds completest sway. No dungeon of Venice or Rome or Naples ever vied with Carolina prisons or Alabama plantations in the excrutiating cruelty which the helpless victims of their fear and hate receive at their hands. When the secrets of this prison house shall be revealed, you will cease to wonder at the tortures of Messina and Palermo. No woman suffered there, only a few score of men. Here tenderest women suffer such cruelty daily, as hard-hearted heathen Rome, the most cruel of the ancient nations, would have shrunk from inflicting. Read Olmstead's late "Tour Through the Back Country," and you will find incidents of these tortures, inflicted so coolly and carelessly, as show them to be a common matter of daily and indifferent outrage. But he never saw the slave roasting at the stake. He never saw the fierce bloodhounds tearing in pieces the tender flesh of fainting women. He never saw, as a friend of mine did, himself once a slaveholder, a frantic mother torn from a nursing babe, less than a year old, and dragged shrieking down the public street of a Missouri village, by men who bore Christian names, and a white skin, and were, not unlikely, born in Puritan New England of pious parents.

> "On horror's head horrors accumulate,"

and the longer we dwell on the dreadful theme, the longer we seem to wish to dwell. It has an awful fascination about it, like the hungry, basilisk gaze of the anaconda. "It holds us with its glittering eye," and we only escape by a strong effort of the will. We emerge from the dungeon so full of

> "Horrid shapes and shrieks and sights unholy,"

and breathe the upper air of liberty, as an angel might feel who had escaped from Pandemonium revelry and outrage into the pure society of the blessed. Alas, unlike the angel, we do not leave only sinners and damned spirits behind us, rioting in their willing wickedness, but pure and lovely souls, pure as the spirits of the just made perfect, lovely as their angels, who do always behold the face of their Father which is in heaven,—these we leave behind, suffering such shame, such sorrow, such anguish of body and of soul as only God can feel, only He can relieve, only He can avenge.

Thank God, that worse than hell shall be swept from the earth. The Administration may not, will not, directly, aid it. The party in power is forbidden to do it, rightfully, constitutionally forbidden. It can only be done peacefully and properly by themselves. It will be so done. The warm air of freedom gliding over all that icy region will relax, will dissolve these chains. The great example of eighteen States of the confederacy, voluntarily emancipating their slaves, or voluntarily endorsing the act by which the nation rescued their domain from its polluting presence, will not be lost upon them. They have lost the post of Master. They will soon be willing to take that of a pupil. They will begin to see as they are seen. They have pompously proclaimed to the despised North, "I am rich and increased with goods and have need of nothing." They will now see that they are "wretched, and miserable, and poor, and blind, and naked." They will then come to that state of humility which will incline them to buy of us "gold tried in the fire," the gold of universal emancipation, "that they may be rich, and white raiment," the wedding robes of liberty and holiness, "that they may be clothed, and that the shame of their nakedness do not appear." "They will anoint their eyes with the eye salve" of northern prosperity, "and will see." Thus learning, thus seeing, the generous spirits that now pant speechless in that prison of silence and death, will give their heart a tongue. The free, white, ruling South will speak every where and speak one voice. Tokens of such coming utterance are already given. North Carolina has spoken through the lips of Mr. Helper and Professor Hedrick ; South Carolina hailed this reform, at its inauguration, in the persons of her Grimkés and Brisbane, and in this very canvass, Professor Lieber, late of her University has boldly denounced her treason and its cause, and cast his vote

for freedom. Kentucky and Virginia already pour forth consent
ing voices, like the volume and the sound of many waters, while
Missouri and Delaware are upon the verge of planting the standard
of emancipation on the summit of their capitols.

This revival of Jeffersonian, of Washingtonian abolitionism, with
more than the fervor and with more than the practical purpose of
those reformers, on their own soil and among their own posterity,
will sweep through the masses, and one fire blaze in all breasts,
—the celestial fire of universal liberty. The struggles of the enslaved, their sufferings, their deaths for personal freedom, not
infrequent and not powerless even now, will increase, and increase
the zeal of their generous advocates; and ere the hundredth anni-
versary of our nation's birth is reached,—the Fourth of July,
1876,—we shall have completed the work undertaken.at our beginning. The bell that rung out the first birthday in the ears of
all the nations, will ring out its first centennial with the prophetic
words inscribed upon it,—"*Proclaim Liberty throughout all the
land to* ALL *the inhabitants thereof;*"—no longer prophecy, to be
accomplished by a long and perilous and bloody path, but blessed,
unchanging history.

We have given it a long lease of power, brief as it may appear
to you, in allowing four Presidential terms to pass before it dis-
appears. But we know that three thousand millions of property
are not to be destroyed in an instant, except by a bloody uprising.
We hope and pray that there may be no such reprisals. It may
go down by a bloodless revolution. Garibaldi has shown how
nearly bloodless an insurrection may be in this age of the world.
Had there been no standing armies in Sicily and Naples. they
would have achieved their liberty without the sacrifice of a single
life. There are no standing armies in the Slave States. A Garibaldi, from the enslaved race, may secure their liberation without
the shedding of a drop of blood. God grant that it may be so.'

---

* The statement of Mr. Buchanan, in his late message, that the slaves are
becoming " uneasy," is a most remarkable confession of a most important witness.
This uneasiness exists more in the Gulf States than on the border. For the latter
gets rid of its dangerous element through the two outlets of Southern trade and
the underground railroad. These Northern slaves, that have been sold South,
because they were unmanagable, are united with the superior native slaves of that

But we look more to the liberal action of the white race than to any violent action of the black. We shall see the sentiment of the States gradually changing. Then their policy will change. Law after law, the worst, first, will be repealed; until, under one grand impulse of conscience, they will pull down the whole fabric, and the slave shall stand beside his master, his free and acknowledged equal.

All this will not take place without such commotion as we have not yet seen nor dreamed of. Threats of disunion, and probably a brief indulgence in that suicidal remedy, will be made by the more insane of the maniacs. We have seen some agitation at the North, in the last thirty years, some mobs and murders have desecrated the free States, in their endeavors to relieve themselves from the *influence* alone of slavery. What will not that bloody power do in a life and death struggle which is now to arise in its own dominions, where it has held unquestioned and unlimited sway for two hundred years? The war has passed from the North to the South, and the thirty thousand votes just cast there for liberty, show that the war will not cease, come what may, fall who may, till that twelve millions are delivered from their few hundred thousand masters, and freedom of every kind, for every man, shall be the glad possession of the whole people.

This must be the work of time. Yet the change is rapid from day-break to dawn; more rapid and brief from dawn to sunrise. And when the sun rises, darkness flees to its caves, though a few shadows may linger among the rays till the mid-day brightness burns them up. So will it be with this cause. The day is breaking. A grey light streaks across the darkened heavens. The next Presidential election will bring the rosy dawn that will send its warm flush athwart the whole horizon. The third will be the perfect sunrise. The fourth the noon-tide glory, that shall

section, who, if on the border, would escape to Canada. These violent and restless men, kept from liberty by a wall five hundred miles thick, will, in time, in the very nature of things, rise upon their masters. These masters, by their madness, are tempting the insurrection. There is the fire, there the powder. If an explosion comes, it will come there first. God grant, the masters may escape the terrible danger by immediate preparation for ultimate, if not instant, emancipation.

consume every ray of slavery blackness that has laid so thick and heavy across the nation's sky.

Let us rejoice. Let us shout for joy. Oppression shall not always reign. Oppression has ceased to reign in its highest, strongest seat. It will soon abandon its lower thrones of State sovereignty, cast down headlong by the people whom it has so long deluded and betrayed. It will then flee from those private, domestic seats of tyranny, upon the multitude of which, the fifteen seats of State authority have been erected, upon which fifteen, faithfully knit together, the throne of their national power has been elevated. An aroused people will extirpate it from these obscure, but central seats, and the gigantic sin that swells vast to heaven, will flee from the earth to its native, nethermost hell.

Let us pray for this hour ; let us labor for it in all righteous and loving ways. Our real work is just begun. We have only broken down a barrier that opposed our march. That march must yet be made. We have only compelled the haughty transgressors to listen. Our entreaties, our warnings, our encouragements are yet to be poured into the opened ear. We have only attained the outmost edge of the broad table land of free discussion. The high land must yet be travelled. Remember that this deed is nothing unless it bring forth fruit better than itself. The object upon which we must fix our eye, the prize that must be won, the goal that must be reached, is the *abolition of slavery,* THE LIBERATION OF EVERY SLAVE.

Let us discuss, in a spirit of prudence and liberality, every measure that seeks this end. Let us bring every reason that worldly success, humane sentiment or religious obligation can suggest to bear upon the hearts of their masters. Let us aid those who are anxious to be released from this relation out of the abundant wealth of the North, that they may not be kept from this duty by the gaunt form of poverty staring them in the face, and certain to be their portion, if they strip themselves of all their inherited, though unrighteous possessions. Let us, at least, assist them, if they need, or will receive no remuneration for the discharge of their duty, by providing for these emancipated brethren a home on free soil, which they cannot enjoy on the slave. We

5

must bring our money to bear upon this sin, if we would see it
peacefully die. Let us do it wisely, generously, speedily.*

Let us especially feel for the slave. The lot, the loss of the
master is nothing to his. His is a hapless, horrible fate. Never
forget him. In your morning prayers remember him upon whom
the morning breaks, only to light him to his rewardless tasks.
When gathering round the family altar and the family table, pity
those who have no such comforts. At your evening devotions
pray for those who go to cheerless couches, bowed down with
dreadful memories and more dreadful fears. Remember that the
Lord had these sufferers before him, no less than his chosen people, when he said, "This is a people robbed and peeled ; they
are all of them snared in holes, and they are hid in prison
houses; they are for a prey, and none delivereth ; for a spoil,
and none saith, *Restore!*" Never, never forget them. They are
your brothers and sisters. They shall stand in equal liberty with
you, delivered by the right arm of Him who saved your fathers,
and who has just cast down their leagued oppressors from their
lofty seats.

What a day that day of deliverance will be,—the great and
acceptable day of the Lord ;—a day sure to come ; a day, I believe, soon to come. Behold that vast and beautiful region, from
the peaceful Ohio to the sunny Gulf, from the swift Mississippi to
the raging Atlantic, as it now rests under the gloom of this awful
sin. All the refinements, all the enterprises of civilized life pause
at its borders, or creep feebly through it like solitary star-rays
through midnight clouds. The magnificent landscape is rarely
cheered with the flying train, rarely adorned with the lovely ham-
let, the prosperous village, the mighty city. The church lifts but
seldom its defiled hand to heaven, and lifts that hand only to
point to the judgment of God on its fearful sin in compelling the
bride of Christ to commit adultery with Belial. No school-house
appears, full of the neighborhood's children, no farms trodden by
their humble, but independent owners ; no culture, prosperity,
piety. The sight most frequent, is the miserable slave toiling

with barbaric implements in the rudest forms of menial service; or the more miserable white man, degraded beneath the slave he despises, idle, intemperate, ignorant, ill-mannered.

Thus stands that vast land to-day. Let the hour come for which we are praying and laboring, to which the great deed of the past week has made the grandest stride that the century has seen; let but that hour come, when every man shall be free, and how changed the spectacle. The wilderness, that blossoms like the rose in wild fertility, shall be transformed into the smiling abode of free, industrious, intelligent man. Railroads shall rush through every valley, bearing the famishing of all nations to the rich treasures nature has there in store for them. Beautiful roads will wind beside every stream, scale every mountain, pierce every forest. Rich embowered cottages, such as no northern sun or soil can give, will line every pathway, will cluster in frequent centres, will multiply, at brief intervals, into great communities, with the great factories, and great warehouses, and spacious stores, and crowded streets of growing cities. The school-house, modest or majestic, as it stands in village or city, will be filled with the young of all families, white and black, as with us, unconscious of difference or prejudice; alike growing in knowledge and affection. No slave whip whistles through the resisting air, rushing down upon the shrinking flesh of saintly woman. No agonizing husbands and wives, mothers and babes, are dragged to the market-place, and there torn, husband from wife, mother from child, never to meet again till they appear together as witnesses on the stand at the bar of God against these murderers of their liberty, their love, their life. No gangs of men and women, silent and sad, move monotonously over the broad acres, to the ceaseless look and lash of the cruel overseer. No wretched hovel, with its earthen floor and heap of straw, filled for a few short hours with the half-starved slaves, blotches the lovely landscape. All these are gone, and gone forever.

The white fields shall blossom under the free and active industry of every class. Comfort shall gladden every home. Willing labor shall garner the land. The free and happy, busy and populous, wealthy and cultivated North shall cover the whole land,

and equal freedom and happiness, energy and prosperity, culture and piety, will be the possession of every man. Above all, the Church of Christ, the Divine Liberator, will point its sacred finger to the Infinite Lover and Redeemer of all men, to the everlasting freedom of heaven. In its walls, without distinction of color or condition, without negro pews, or negro galleries, or negro corners, all souls shall bow in the loving unity of " one Lord, one faith, one baptism," before " the one God and Father of all, who is above all, and through all, and in all" that love Him, equally and eternally.

No dim and distant prophecy of millennial glory is this. The day is nigh at hand. It has already dawned. It shall speedily arise. " Surely I come *quickly*. Amen! Even so, come, Lord Jesus!"

APPENDIX.

———◆———

A.

BUNKER'S HILL AND HARPER'S FERRY.

THE analogy between these two historic events has been suggested by several speakers and writers. It has not been as carefully elaborated as it deserves to be, and will be by future historians. It may not be amiss to state a few of the points of resemblance they will detect, both in respect to the enterprises themselves, and their real leaders.

They are not unlike in rashness, viewed in the light of cool, sagacious generalship. Consider the former. Fifteen hundred untrained soldiers, with only four rounds apiece of cartridge and ball, planted themselves behind a mere bank of turf and sticks, thrown up in less than twelve hours, within a few rods of a ship channel, where the enemy's men-of-war lay, and whence they could rake them on three sides, and cut off their retreat on the fourth. Consider, farther, that a great city was less than a mile distant, full of ammunition and of thoroughly trained soldiers, and its nearest eminence, in height and distance, commanded their site as perfectly as though it had been perched over their heads but a rood off. Is there greater military wisdom in putting such a handful of raw militia into such a trap, than Capt. Brown showed in his operations? Wellington or Washington would have never undertaken the former any sooner than the latter.

If we look at each of them, as they appeared to the hopes or even the dreams of Warren and of Brown, we shall find them not dissimilar. No historian ever has clearly set forth the immediate practical good that the encampment on Bunker's Hill was intended, or desired to effect;—we doubt if they ever will. It could not have been dreamed for a moment, that their position could be retained for any length of time. Without shelter, without rocky ramparts, or means to erect them, without ammunition, or cannon, or provision, shut off from all communication with the main army as completely as if in a besieged fortress, they could not have hoped for any thing but a bloody battle, fruitless in its immediate results, even if successful, or a final submission of the whole force by the slow, but, in this case, most certain process of siege. Had not the British been rash with rage and pride, they could have had the whole fifteen hundred in their hands in less than a week, without the loss of a man, as easily as the Virginians could have starved Capt. Brown into surrender, had they too, had the grace of patience. It may be said the Americans made a blunder, and located themselves nearer Boston, and on a lower hill than they intended. So the leader of the Harper's Ferry enterprise said he made a blunder, and did not follow any of his plans in entering the arsenal. History will give them both the benefits of their claim, if she gives either. What then? The hill they intended to occupy is just as completely shut off from the camp, as the one they fortified. It has only one advantage over the latter. This one, is overtopped by Copp's Hill in Boston, that one, not. It is, however, within reach of its fire, as well as that of the fleet. The mountains on which Brown said he meant to establish himself, are not subject to like objection. The enterprise of Putnam, Prescott and Warren, has not any such claim to real necessity as must be allowed to the fight at Lexington and the fortification of Dorchester Heights. It was a *trial* battle. It would have always been branded as criminally foolish, but for the higher than strategetical, or so called practical reasons, which incited it, and especially but for the wonderful fruits it brought forth in the hearts of friends and foes. Will not the future historian of the great conflict of slavery and freedom find like analogies in the events of Harper's Ferry? In one respect we pray and believe they will totally differ. The former was the prelude of a long and cruel civil war. The latter, we hope, will prove to be the only bloody interruption to the peaceable progress of this cause. It will certainly have this relation, if the slave masters learn more wisdom from this event than our British masters did from Bunker's Hill.

We cannot fail to notice the remarkable resemblance of the real leaders of these enterprises, both in respect to their own temperament, as well as in their relation to their associates in the general movement. Warren differed as much from the other great leaders in the cause of liberty then, as John Brown did from those of to-day. His voice was fierce for war long before the others considered the argument of peace exhausted. His deeds were like his words. On the Lexington day, he was fighting in the ranks, while Hancock and Samuel Adams, equally great patriots, and esteemed by the king far more dangerous rebels, felt it their duty to seek safety in flight. His rash courage almost sealed his fate that day. For at West Cambridge a ball passed so near his head as to carry away the pin that fastened his earlock. Had he been captured at Bunker's Hill, as he undoubtedly would have been but for the fortunate stab of a bayonet, he would, most certainly, have been hung within a month on Boston Common, by the Governor of Massachusetts, for " murder, treason, and inciting to insurrection."

There are only two points of difference between these transactions. The first, that those who fought were, in the one case, themselves the victims of the oppression: in the other, chiefly sympathizers with these victims. This is not quite true, though constantly asserted. For colored men, free and slave, were engaged at Harper's Ferry. Some were slain, some escaped, some were captured and hung. It was planned and perfected, theoretically, among the fugitives of Canada. Col. Washington's favorite slave was among the slain, and no one knows, no one can know, till slavery is abolished, how great an army was pledged to meet at the rendezvous in the mountains.

The second point of difference is, that much legislative and military preparation preceded the former encounter, none, the latter. It will be noticed, in connection with this fact, that the ruling government of Massachusetts had allowed, for many years, mass meetings, congresses, petitions of its subjects, the collection of military stores, and, at last, permitted 14,000 of these rebels to be encamped under arms within three miles of its capitol. Suppose Virginia had granted its subjects such privileges, would they not have developed civil and military leaders, and executed enterprises of great pith and moment, without the aid of a foreign arm? Let us reflect that history, which is the voice of humanity, never takes into account, in its ultimate and irreversible judgment, immediate success or failure. The *final cause* rules here as every where. Warren and Bunker's Hill are still, and ever will be, the most thrilling names of the Revolutionary struggle. Those to whose liberty they are dedicated, have compelled all nations to do them reverence, by their own unceasing, enthusiastic devotion. So the like, yet far greater admiration of the Afric-American race, when they shall have achieved their freedom, will compel all the world to revere the names of John Brown and Harper's Ferry. Their representative shall yet stand with the descendant of John Brown and the successor of Governor Wise, in mutual amity and grateful reverence before a commemorative monument at Harper's Ferry, as the descendants of George the Third and Joseph Warren lately stood, with the representative of emancipated Massachusetts, cordial and reverent, before the sacred memorials of Bunker's Hill.

B.

A MANUMISSION AID SOCIETY—THE RIGHT WAY TO ABOLISH SLAVERY.

We take the liberty of reprinting a part of a letter, which was sent to the Tremont Temple Convention of Dec. 3d. It developes, somewhat fully, the idea advanced on page 34, and urges what seems to us the most imperative and immediate duty of all who love the slave and his master :—

the employment of the immense private wealth of the country for their mutual salvation. We commend it to the earnest consideration of all those who are willing to pay as well as pray, for the extinction of slavery.

* * * * * * * *

It has long been my opinion that slavery would not die bloodlessly, unless the moneyed power was brought to bear against it. All other forces are largely immaterial. They address the conscience, the sympathies, the fears, the abstract political relations of the slaveholder. This is primarily and pre-eminently material. Every body can understand what it means and what it does. Other powers expend themselves in words of denunciation, resolution or legislation, all alike costless and most of them, practically, useless. The bestowing of our goods to ransom the poor slave will appeal directly to the sympathies of the master and summon him to similar, and even greater sacrifices. Other activities awaken the bitterest opposition ; this disarms all hostility. For the warmest friend of slavery cannot become enraged at the generous sacrifice of private property for its extinction. Finally, by arraying the vast moneyed power in the right way and in the right spirit against this evil, we shall bring the least and greatest of its foes to one act, and thus gradually to one feeling, in respect to all the other right modes of assailing it, and so hasten the glad hour of universal emancipation.

How then shall the wealth of the North be brought to bear directly against slavery ? Different minds will answer this question differently. Some will say by colonization movements to Africa, Hayti, or Central America. Others will say by national taxation for the purchase of the so-called property. Without discussing these views, or those of any other philanthropists, allow me to say that, in my opinion, this can be most easily obtained and most effectively used by *organizing a society, which shall secure to emancipated slaves, homes in the free States, which they cannot now have in the slave ; and shall also offer to the master, if he is unable or unwilling to gratuitously liberate them—a slight remuneration for his great pecuniary sacrifice.* In a word, we want, A MANUMISSION AID SOCIETY.

Permit me to notice these two points a little more in detail :

First, We need a society that shall provide homes for those who would be emancipated, were it not for the laws, almost universal in the slave States, which forbid their manumission on the soil. The cases of conscience are not infrequent, even in the present reign of terror, of masters who are giving their slaves their liberty. In Maryland, between the time of the enactment of the law last winter forbidding the emancipation of slaves, and the fourth of last July, when it was to go into effect, between eighty and ninety slaves were set at liberty, in one county alone. Masters not unfrequently appear with their servants in our northern courts to execute the deed of manumission. If a few thus obey their conscience under all their impediments, social, religious and legal, would not many do it, if there was a responsible society to encourage them, by receiving their slaves and giving them a comfortable home, and a fair start in life?

Those who are most moved to this duty have the most regard for their slaves. Many of them are ignorant of the North. Many have no means of giving them an outfit in addition to their liberty. They cannot drive them into unknown and inhospitable regions. Hence, they pause in their ignorance and anxiety, and too often sink back into indifference, and die in that state, leaving their slaves to their fate. *A Manumission Aid Society* would remove all these natural objections, arouse the slumbering consciences, and meet with a hearty response from a large class of convicted slaveholders. It will find a home for the slaves, either here or abroad, as might seem best in each case. It will meet the kind hearted master, for all *such* masters are kind hearted, with deeds that will speak more forcibly than all our words possibly can.

But a second benefit resulting from such a society, will be the material aid it will afford to those masters who are almost persuaded to liberate their slaves, and who are restrained by the thought that the deed will utterly impoverish them. We want a society that shall say to these penitent slave-holders, " If you will not give up your slaves without some help, we will give you that help. We do not recognize your title to them. We, simply as a charity to you, give you a little out of our wealth, or out of our poverty, as would most frequently be the case, to aid you in following your conscience whither it now leads you." We should prefer, and, as far as possible, secure, their gratuitous liberation. But the salvation of the poor slave, so near his liberty and which he can reach by so slight a donation on our part, ought to urge us to this benevolence. Let us remove the chief, almost the only stumbling block that lies in the way of the duty of conscientious masters—the fear of poverty. This has been done again and again, in the temperance movement. It has in this. One of our greatest philanthropists and abolitionists informed me that on one occasion he ransomed ten slaves for $1000, and on another, five slaves by paying $100. Let all anti-slavery men, through a responsible society, imitate this excellent example, and they will find hundreds of masters equally, yea, more liberal than these, who so generously responded to his generous offers.

Many lesser yet not unimportant benefits might be named. Allow me to trespass a little farther on your time by mentioning one or two of them : First, such a society would relieve us of almost all of our present private donations for the purchase of slaves, which if they could be ascertained, would be found to amount to a vast sum. Much of this is obtained under false pretences, much of it is fruitless through failure to collect the amount required, and all of it very costly. For every one so liberated, ten to twenty, possibly twice these numbers, could be set free through this society.

42

Another very important benefit would be the union of the anti-slavery sentiment on a practical and effective basis. The late election reveals the fact that only six hundred thousand, out of four and a half million of voters, are bound, body and soul, to slavery. However feebly the anti-slavery feeling moves in the breasts of many of the remaining three millions and nine hundred thousand, it exists there, and such a society would do more to develope it than any other instrumentality.

But if we take Mr. Lincoln's vote alone, and join with it the abolitionists, whose conscience forbade their supporting him, we shall have nearly, if not quite, two millions of men, who are directly, and, most of them, strongly opposed to slavery. Cannot this great multitude be united in a voluntary, practical measure for its abolition? No such measure seems to me to be before the country; none, certainly, that will enlist their purses as well as their hearts. Politicians are almost as cautious as financiers. The party coming into power is prevented from any direct efforts to abolish slavery. Cannot a society be organized in which all can constitutionally, earnestly, liberally work? Will not this society afford that basis?

It may be said emancipation, by purchase, is no new idea. We acknowledge it; if it were, we should doubt its wisdom. It has often been said that compensation must be given for the slaves; but it has always, so far as I am aware, been said that such compensation should be given by the general or local governments to the local governments:—Congress or the free States treating with the slave States, or the slave holders, as a mass. Mr. Webster advocated appropriating the proceeds of the Public Lands for this object. Mr. Seward advocated buying up the slaves in the District of Columbia, with the consent of all the masters, by appropriations from the national treasury. Rev. Dr. Bangs, and within a few years, Mr. Burritt, have advocated special taxation for this purpose. Rev. Dr. Thomson, in the Christian Advocate and Journal, and Mr. Thurlow Weed, in the Albany Journal, have lately advanced similar ideas. All of these are misled by the English mode of abolishing slavery. Our governments, local or national, unlike the European governments, rarely engage in works of pure benevolence. They help them, but they do not institute or maintain them. This is done almost exclusively by voluntary societies. All of our religious, and almost all of our charitable and higher educational movements, are managed by such organizations. The peculiarity of the idea we advocate is, that it conforms to these habits and tastes of our people. It is a voluntary society, like the American Colonization or Kansas Aid Societies, both of which have been aided by State appropriations.

Let it once enter the list of our charities, and it would speedily surpass them all. Scores of men and women will be found in every village, hundreds in every city, who will collect moneys for its treasury, and will assist in securing for the slaves that come into its hands, pleasant and prosperous

homes. Money would pour into its coffers from all classes, from those of
every shade of opinion.

The greatest of these voluntary charities, the American Bible Society,
has an annual income of about $450,000. But this society has not a tithe
of the hold upon the hearts of the people, nor can it elicit but a fraction of
the support that a Manumission Aid Society, rightly organized and officered,
could command. Yet consider how powerful a society would be, receiving,
as a free gift, such an annual income as this, and expending it in the ransom of slaves and their home or foreign colonization. But such a society
would have a much larger income than this. No Legislature, State or National, aids the Bible Society. They would all aid one devoted to the
cause of voluntary emancipation. Mr. Everett, who has by his eloquence
rescued the home of Washington from infamy, would be imitated by hundreds of orators, laboring to rescue the land of Washington from far deeper
infamy. Perhaps he would himself lead these followers in this noblest of
enterprises. If each of the two millions of avowed opponents of slavery
give an average of one dollar per annum, for its peaceful extinction, we
should have two millions of dollars for annual disbursement. We believe a
larger income than this could be secured : for multitudes, South as well as
North, slaveholders and non-slaveholders, who would not vote directly
against slavery, would gladly aid in such an effort to exterminate it. Thus,
with abundant means at command, it would rapidly eliminate the conscientious masters from their more violent and wicked associates, and even these
bitter enemies of freedom, melted by our large liberality, would cease to
rage, cease to resist, until finally, all conspiring together, the South and the
North, by private and public charity, by State and National appropriations,
the great iniquity shall be lifted from every neck, and all sit in freedom
and happiness under the equal protection of justice and liberty. Lest this
estimate should appear extravagant, allow me to quote an extract from Mr.
Emerson's speech in New York, in 1856. By inserting the word "Society" for "State," we have the very idea of this association, and an eloquent
statement of its means and results.

"Why, in the name of common sense and the peace of mankind, is not
the summary or gradual abolition of slavery, in accordance with the inter-
ests of the South and the settled conscience of the North, made the subject
of instant negotiation and settlement ? Because it is property ? Then it
has a price. It is not a really great task to buy that property of the
planter. I say, buy, never conceding the right of the planter to own, but
acknowledging the calamity of his position and willing to bear a country-
man's share in relieving him, and because it is *the only practicable* course,
and is innocent. [Loud applause.] Was there ever any contribution so
enthusiastically paid as this will be ? Every man will bear his part. We
will give up our coaches, and wine and watches. The church will melt its
plate. The Father of his country shall wait, well pleased, a little longer
for his monument. Franklin shall wait for his, the Pilgrim Fathers for
theirs, and Columbus, who waited all his mortality for justice, shall wait a

part of his immortality also. We will call upon those rich beneficiaries who found asylums, hospitals, Lowell institutes and Astor libraries, upon wealthy bachelors and wealthy maidens, to make the State [Society] their heirs, as they were wont to do at Rome. The rich shall give of their riches, the merchants of their commerce, the mechanics their strength; the needle women will give, and the children will have a cent society. Every man in the land would give a week's work to dig away this accursed mountain of slavery, and force it forever out of the world."

These views are submitted with the hope that they will aid in the peaceful settlement of the most important and most difficult question that is before the age.

www.ingramcontent.com/pod-product-compliance
Lightning Source LLC
Chambersburg PA
CBHW021440090426

42739CB00009B/1566